Original title:
Tidings of Christmas Joy

Copyright © 2024 Creative Arts Management OÜ
All rights reserved.

Author: Rory Fitzgerald
ISBN HARDBACK: 978-9916-94-104-1
ISBN PAPERBACK: 978-9916-94-105-8

A Celebration of Light and Love

Snowflakes fall, the lights do twinkle,
Laughter echoes, with each jolly sprinkle.
Socks mismatched, we dance around,
In our holiday chaos, joy is found.

Hot cocoa spills, the marshmallows float,
Grandma's fruitcake? We won't gloat.
Family hugs and goofy grins,
In this warm haze, where silliness wins.

Gifts of the Heart Unwrapped

Unwrap the laughter, it's quite the sight,
A grandpa's sweater, oh what a fright!
Batteries missing? Oh what a tease,
Remember last year? More laughter than cheese.

Toys that squeak, they drive the dog mad,
Yet under the tree, it's still not so bad.
With every mishap, our spirits do lift,
The best present of all is the gift of a gift.

Frosty Love Notes on the Window

Frosty patterns hide the view,
But our kids wrote love notes, that much is true.
Snowball fights, Oh what a blast,
With laughter in flakes, our hearts are amassed.

Wipe the windows, see the fun,
Snowmen grinning, they're number one.
Each silly mishap becomes a new tale,
As we sip on eggnog and giggle without fail.

Sprigs of Evergreen and Unity

Evergreen branches, what a delight,
Except when they scratch, in the middle of night.
Deck the halls, let the pets run free,
Dancing around in pure jubilee.

Cookies all baked, they're now just crumbs,
The cat got in, and look what it becomes!
The spirit of laughter fills every nook,
As we gather 'round for our holiday book.

A Nest of Joy Amidst the Chill

Snowflakes fall with silly grace,
Hot cocoa spills all over the place.
We build a snowman, quite a sight,
He melts away, oh what a fright!

Grandma dances with her cat,
Socks on wrong, imagine that!
The tree leans like it's had too much,
Yet laughter warms us with its touch.

Echoes of Laughter Through Time

Uncle Joe tells tales so tall,
The turkey gobbles; it might just squall.
A gift from Auntie, oh what luck!
It's just a sweater with a duck!

The kids all giggle, hide, and seek,
While the dog steals the holiday feast.
We swear it's merry, no time for woe,
Just laugh till you roll, that's the show!

Serendipity Under a Blanket of Snow

Carols sung off-key with glee,
A cat in the tree, oh what a spree!
Mittens lost and found in the fridge,
What's that smell? Did someone smudge?

Snowball fights, a slippery race,
Dad face-plants, oh, what a place!
With laughter erupting all around,
In this winter, oh joy is found!

The Quiet Joy of Togetherness

Sipping cocoa while dad snores loud,
A bickering squirrel steals the crowd.
Presents wrapped by a three-legged dog,
Uncle's snoring? A real holiday fog!

Grandma's knitting is quite a sight,
Yarn balls rolling, what a delight!
With hugs and giggles, here we stay,
Family fun in our own strange way!

Whispers of Winter Wonder

Snowflakes dance like clumsy ghosts,
Frogs in toques and sticky toast.
Elves trip over candy canes,
While reindeer hide from frosty rains.

Hot cocoa spills while sleds go zoom,
Chasing snowmen with vacuum gloom.
A snowball fight breaks out in glee,
As penguins waddle, silly and free.

Echoes of Festive Cheer

Santa's stuck, he's lost his sleigh,
While kids sing loudly, 'Hip-hip-hooray!'
Rudolph sneezes, lighting the way,
As gingerbread men begin to sway.

Festive sweaters with funny prints,
Grandma's casserole makes everyone squint.
The cat is tangled in bright string lights,
While the tree leans, ready for fights.

Sparkles in the Frost

Icicles sparkle like frozen spears,
While frostbitten noses bring on the cheers.
Laughter echoes through winter's embrace,
As snowmen wear scarves from last summer's race.

Frosty mornings with giggles galore,
Kids racing sleds while parents snore.
Chasing snowflakes, they slip and glide,
Turning the yard into a silly ride.

The Spirit of Giving

Gift wrap battles leave paper trails,
Pups in bows create epic fails.
A fruitcake thrown across the room,
Mom's baked cookies go boom, bang, boom!

Picking names from a goofy hat,
Grandpa's sweater, a funny cat.
An awkward dance around the tree,
With every twist, pure jubilee!

A Chronicle of Celebrated Moments

In a kitchen filled with laughter,
A turkey does a little dance,
Grandma's secret recipe fails,
And the dog tries a food romance.

The lights twinkle like fireflies,
Uncle Joe wears a silly hat,
A cat jumps right on the table,
To claim the feast, just how 'bout that?

Stockings stuffed with socks and treats,
A toddler raises his delight,
He thinks Santa's on a diet,
But the cookie crumbs tell the plight.

With jokes that barely make them grin,
And games that spiral into fun,
This merry band of quirky folks,
Make each year a crazy run.

Boughs of Holly and Wishes for All

Boughs of holly hang askew,
The tree leans like it's half asleep,
Cousin Tim's on the floor again,
With ornaments in quite a heap.

We sing off-key, but with great cheer,
Dad's rendition of that old tune,
The cat leaps up, steals the show,
While the dog hums a funny croon.

Presents wrapped in duct tape shine,
A gift for dad, a toy for me,
The kids all giggle when they see,
The sock that's labeled, 'Gift from Flea.'

But amidst the chaos, warmth is here,
In laughter shared and playful jest,
These moments, wacky but sincere,
Becoming memories we love best.

The Laughter of Children at Play

Snowmen wobble, hats askew,
Kids are giggling, a wild crew.
Sleds are racing down the hill,
With every bump, a scream, a thrill.

Mittens mismatched, boots untied,
Slide on ice, oh what a ride!
Snowballs flying, laughter loud,
Winter's joy, a jolly crowd.

Bright Reflections in the Winter Chill

Faces glowing, cheeks so red,
Hot cocoa talks are often said.
Frosty windows, crazy sights,
Icicles hanging, winter bites.

Shovels clatter, oh what fun!
Throw a snowball, just get it done!
Laughter echoing down the street,
While snowflakes fall, oh so sweet.

A Time for Giving and Grace

Cookies made with extra sprinkles,
Charades played with silly wrinkled.
Gifts wrapped tight, oh what a mess,
Ribbons tangled in a tussle, yes!

Jolly Santa makes his rounds,
With reindeer stomping on rooftops' grounds.
Funny socks and silly hats,
Unwrap the laughs, then share with cats.

The Dance of Snowflakes in Flight

Snowflakes swirling, a playful dive,
Falling like confetti, oh, alive!
Catch one quick, it's gone in a blink,
Nature's giggles, don't you think?

Dance like no one's watching, twirl,
Embrace the flurry, give it a whirl!
With frosty breath and joyful squeals,
Winter's humor spins on wheels.

Sparkling Lights and Warm Embraces

The tree's lit up like a disco ball,
With ornaments that wobble and fall.
A cat takes aim, a playful glance,
In soft pjs, we all dance.

Eggnog spills on the carpet bright,
As we juggle cookies with all our might.
A pie's gone missing, oh what a sight,
Laughter echoes deep into night.

A Chorus of Joyful Hearts

Singing loudly with off-key cheer,
The neighbors peek in, eyes full of fear.
Mistletoe hangs, yet no one dares,
To pucker up in these silly flares.

The cards we send, a wild mix,
With bad selfies, it's quite the fix.
In matching sweaters, hugs abound,
A kooky family joyfully found.

Memories Wrapped in Silver and Gold

Unwrapping gifts with great delight,
It's the giant box that gives a fright.
Inside a sweater that's two sizes too large,
We laugh and joke how it's a barrage.

The cookies burn, the smoke alarm blares,
We cough and chuckle without any cares.
Each mishap adds to our lore so bold,
In laughter's warmth, our hearts unfold.

When Angels Sing of Peace

The carolers come, but who's that chasing?
A dog in a wig, so much misplacing!
They serenade, but with lost notes,
It's more a battle of wobbly boats.

With every laugh, our spirits rise,
As we try to gather in goofy disguise.
Together we sway, in joy so deep,
Creating memories, a whimsy to keep.

Heartbeats of Holiday Harmony

In socks too big, the cat's on the floor,
He pounces at shadows, then snores evermore.
Uncle Joe's sweater, so bright and so bold,
He wears it with pride, like a story retold.

Cookies are burned, but we still have some fun,
We laugh and we dance, just for everyone's pun.
The tree's leaning right, thanks to dogs on the roam,
It's a wobbly sight, but we still feel at home.

Lanterns in the Midnight Sky

Stars in the sky look like sprinkles of glee,
While Grandma's new recipe's gone wild, you see.
Chasing the sparks as they twirl and they spin,
The lights on the house are the best kind of win.

With pickles and eggnog, we toast to good cheer,
And wear silly hats that no one should wear.
The laughter erupts like popcorn in pots,
This holiday madness, we've got in whole lots.

Gatherings of Gratitude and Cheer

A dance-off erupts right in the kitchen,
With mom doing moves that are truly quite glitchin'.
The turkey's still raw, and the dogs run away,
But we'll find some pizza and eat anyway!

A toast with our mugs, full of cocoa and whip,
With marshmallows floating like boats on a trip.
The kids make a mess, it's a grand little scene,
As we sing off-key, feeling jolly and keen.

The Magic of Mistletoe Moments

Under the mistletoe, we giggle and sway,
But Auntie just slips and falls in dismay.
With kisses and laughter, the chaos just grows,
Especially when grandpa starts telling his prose.

The snowmen out front are slightly askew,
That's what we get for a sculptor like you.
With candy cane swords, we battle with glee,
In this wacky old house, it's as fun as can be!

Candles Glowing in the Frost

Candles flicker, oh what a sight,
They dance in shadows, like stars at night.
Frosty windows, our breath like steam,
We giggle and snicker, is this a dream?

Hot cocoa spills, marshmallows afloat,
Sipped too quickly, oh what a gloat!
My sweater's tight, I've eaten a ton,
Unwrap my belly, I'm not even done!

A Tapestry of Warm Memories

Grandma's cookies taste like delight,
Burnt edges? No worries, they're still just right!
Stories spin round like yarn on a spool,
Laughter erupts, we're nobody's fool.

Uncle Joe's tie is a sight to behold,
Riddled with colors, both bright and bold.
We play charades while wearing a grin,
A tangle of joy, let the nonsense begin!

Snowy Walks and Sweet Reminiscing

Snowflakes swirl like they're at a ball,
Slip and slide, oh we're having a fall!
Chasing our shadows, we trip and we tumble,
The laughter erupts, oh how we do rumble.

Frosty noses and cheeks all aglow,
Sledding downhill, oh what a show!
We build up our dreams in a snowman's grin,
Building our hopes in the shivers we're in.

From Pine Cones to Wishes

Pine cones tumble, what a surprise,
Hit me right on the head—oh my, oh my!
Crafting our wishes by the blazing fire,
Singing off-key, yet we never tire.

Decorations hang with a sparkly cheer,
Dad's snoring echoes while we all steer.
A tree that's crooked, it leans to the right,
Just like our plans—oops! It's another night!

Evergreen Dreams

In the forest, trees wear hats,
Dancing squirrels, chasing cats.
Birds are singing, some off-key,
Even the raccoons sip sweet tea.

Jingle bells on every branch,
A frosty deer does a beer dance.
Ornaments hung by the moon's glow,
While the pine trees steal the show.

Snowflakes falling, round and fluffy,
Hot cocoa spills, a little guffy.
Kids in mittens, sliding down,
Rolling snowmen in the town.

With laughter echoing through the night,
Mistletoe swings, quite the sight.
Socks are hung, filled with fun,
This merry season has just begun!

Fireside Whispers

By the fire, we roast marshmallows,
Sticking close, we tell our tales.
Busted toys and socks for gifts,
Everyone giggling at the drifts.

A cat on the mantel, looking sly,
Chasing shadows, oh my oh my!
Grandpa's snoring gives us a scare,
Sleeping through the fun, unaware.

Eggnog spills, oh what a mess,
A dancing elf might just confess.
Silly hats and reindeer games,
We laugh out loud, calling names.

As the logs crackle and pop,
We wish the fun would never stop.
With cheers we raise our cups so high,
Here's to joy that makes us fly!

Chimes of the Season

Bells are ringing, but who is there?
Santa's lost his favorite chair.
With a wink, he dances in socks,
Truth be told, he loves ice blocks.

Frosty makes a run for the door,
Claiming he doesn't need a floor.
Carolers sing, but get the tune wrong,
Making up words, all night long.

The cupcakes frosted, all gone flat,
A reindeer munches on my hat.
The cookie plate is now a sight,
With crumbs that spark a festive light.

As laughter bursts, just like a star,
Even grandma got a guitar.
We strum and sing with all our might,
Embracing joy, oh what a night!

A Starlit Night's Embrace

Look at those lights twinkling bright,
  Wishing the neighbors goodnight.
  Snowmen wave with goofy grins,
  While puppies bark and then spin.

The moon peeks through with a grin,
  As we pull our cozy hats in.
  Mittens mismatched make us jest,
  Here comes the guest, all in jest!

Around the tree, we gather near,
  Spilling secrets, spreading cheer.
  In flannel pajamas, warm and snug,
  We share hot cocoa, oh what a hug.

As the clock strikes a joyful hour,
Shenanigans spring up like a flower.
With hearts so full, we sing so loud,
We are the festive, joy-filled crowd!

The Art of Joyful Giving

Wrap the cat, not my gift,
Watch her squirm, what a rift!
Sticky tape on my nose,
Oh, this chaos just grows!

Grandma's fruitcake in hand,
I swear it's a brick, not planned!
Who thought raisins were cool?
Guess they still rule the school!

A sweater two sizes too wide,
A reindeer that sparkles with pride.
Unwrap the socks, they glow bright,
I'll wear them all on Christmas night!

A gift card expired, oh dear,
But we'll laugh about it with cheer!
This season's a burst of delight,
Let's dance through the festive night!

Starry Nights and Cozy Fires

Under the stars, let's roast treats,
S'mores are epic, but sticky cheeks.
The dog makes off with my bun,
Who knew cooking could be such fun?

The fire crackles, spirits fly,
Log on floor—was that my thigh?
Hot chocolate spills everywhere,
Guess I need a new chair to share!

Elves outside dancing in snow,
One trips and falls—oh, what a show!
We laugh till we snort and wheeze,
Such moments bring us all to ease.

Stars keep twinkling, hearts are light,
Let's make merry all through the night.
With laughter's echo, spirits lift,
Each moment shared is the best gift!

Secrets of the Evergreen Forest

In the forest where whispers dwell,
A squirrel steals cookies—what the heck, oh well!
The trees stand tall, wearing snow,
I swear I saw one punch a crow!

Elves are hiding up in the pines,
Swapping tales over cups of wines.
Fairies giggle, they lose their glow,
Watch out for snowballs—here they go!

A deer in glasses looks so fine,
Sipping cocoa, feeling divine.
Tree ornaments dance in a line,
Who knew forest parties could be so benign?

Underneath branches, laughter trails,
The giggles mix with winter gales.
These secrets shared in nature's nest,
Fill our hearts, we feel so blessed!

The Sound of Joy in Every Corner

Jingle bells play in the hall,
Everyone's dancing, let's have a ball!
But watch the cat, she's on the prowl,
With a leap and a swipe, oh, what a howl!

Grandpa's snoring, loud as a train,
He dreams of hockey—what a vein!
Mistletoe hangs, oh dear, oh shoot,
Kiss that person, now that's the hoot!

Children giggling, wrapped in bright lights,
The puppy chews on their new tights.
Balloons are popping, laughter's spree,
Who knew the chaos could feel so free?

Each corner hums with silly cheer,
Voices raised, a song to hear.
This joyous noise that fills the air,
Is Christmas spirit everywhere!

Hearts Wrapped in Warmth

In a world where cocoa flows,
And the laughter brightly glows,
Santa's sleigh is stuck on roofs,
While dogs chase after little moose!

Families gather, hats askew,
Wearing sweaters that are too blue.
Uncles dance like they just learned,
While grandma's cookies become a fern!

Gifts are wrapped with tape that's thick,
But aunties slipped, oh what a trick!
The tree is leaning, or a bit askew,
Just like that last year's fruitcake stew!

But hearts as big as winter nights,
Spread warmth and cheer, such silly sights.
With each embrace and goofy grin,
The holiday spirit's sure to win!

Joyful Harmonies at Dusk

The kids are caroling off-key,
While the cat sets the tree free!
Pine needles drop like little stars,
As dad starts dancing with the jars!

Neighbors peek from frosty panes,
Hoping to hear those silly refrains.
The choir's pitch just lost a fight,
With grandma's yodeling taking flight!

The lights are twinkling, 'cept for one,
It flickers out and ruins the fun.
Down the block, the snowmen grin,
With carrot noses stuck in their chin!

But laughter spreads through every lane,
Hot chocolate spills, oh what a stain!
In this mess, we all find glee,
A melody shared, just you and me!

A Mistletoe Dream

Underneath that leafy green,
A couple's made a funny scene.
They forgot that quirky shoe,
And bumped their heads while leaning too!

Kisses shared while cats just yawn,
One cheek squished, a hairdryer drawn.
A sudden gust throws mistletoe,
Now everyone wants to join the show!

The parrot squawks with all its might,
As granddad tries to steal a bite.
Laughter echoes through the hall,
With mistletoe hanging, no shame at all!

The night's a mix of joy and cheer,
As laughter dances, draws us near.
In tangled lights and tangled love,
We're all just fools, like stars above!

Snowflakes and Silver Bells

Flakes are falling, dogs in coats,
Kids are chanting silly quotes.
The snowman's grin is a funny sight,
With a carrot nose that's way too tight!

Silver bells ring, oh such delight,
"But who put glitter on my bike?"
Grandma's pies are burnt to the core,
Is it too late to order some more?

Sledding down the hill, what a sight,
One kid flips, while others take flight.
Hot soup's served, but oh dear me,
There's a frog that jumped in with glee!

Yet laughter fills the chilly air,
With every slip and silly scare.
In this chaos, it's clear to see,
The joy of life is meant to be!

Candles and Cocoa Delight

Candles flicker, what a sight,
Marshmallows float, oh so bright.
Sipping cocoa, just for fun,
Whipped cream towers, who needs sun?

Laughter echoes, snowflakes dance,
Hot cocoa spills, a frothy chance.
Sugar cookies, sprinkles galore,
The cat just knocked down the door!

Reindeer slippers, cozy and warm,
Chasing wrappers, oh what charm!
Twinkling lights upon the floor,
My dog thinks it's a festive chore!

Jolly laughter fills the air,
With a snowman in my hair!
Choc'late drips on my new socks,
Who knew joy came in big blocks?

Stars in the Silent Night

Stars are twinkling, just like me,
Dreaming of gifts under the tree.
Elves are wrapping, what a sight,
Found my dog dressed, oh what fright!

Snowmen tumble, hats in dismay,
One rolled down—what a ballet!
Hot chocolate spills, as kids gleefully shout,
"Jump in the snow, we'll cake you out!"

The moon winks down, with a grin,
While reindeer prance with a spin.
Giggles float through the chilly air,
Who'd have thought snow could be such a dare?

With snowball fights and mitten tags,
We'll dodge and dance through all the bags.
Under stars that twinkle bright,
We'll share our snacks in sheer delight!

Memories Wrapped in Ribbons

Ribbons tangled, what a mess,
Unwrapping gifts, such a stress!
Grandma's sweater, two sizes too wide,
Wrapped up snug to hide her pride.

Fragrant cookies, smell so sweet,
Got flour on my nose and feet.
Presents open with joyful screams,
Found my cat stuck in the seams!

Family photos from years gone past,
Laughing at outfits, what a blast!
Hold the moments, memories dear,
With each corner, bring forth cheer.

Silly hats and mismatched socks,
Crazy games that ticked the clocks.
Through laughter shared, and stories told,
It's the warmth of love that we hold.

The Gift of Laughter

Under the tree, a jolly surprise,
A gift of giggles, laughter that flies.
Wrapping paper, a crinkly sound,
Laughter erupts all around.

Whispers of jokes, jokes full of cheer,
Uncle's bad puns, everyone near.
Knocking gifts and silly pranks,
Laughter flows in playful ranks.

Tickles and snorts, oh what a sight,
Sharing old stories late into night.
With ringing laughter filling the space,
In this merry dance, we find our place.

So here's to moments, joyful and bright,
Wrapped in giggles, shared with delight.
In every chuckle and playful tease,
We find the magic, the heart that frees.

Laid in Love and Light

Bells ring out with a silly sound,
Snowmen waddle all around.
Elves get tangled in their lights,
While reindeer dance on winter nights.

Cookies crumble, milk goes splat,
Santa's stuck—oh, what of that?
He laughs as he squeezes through the flue,
Yelling, "Where's the snack? I need my due!"

Mittens lost and scarves a mess,
Snowballs fly, oh what a guess!
Frosty slips and falls with glee,
Joyful chaos for all to see.

Singing songs in silly tones,
Misfit toys make funny groans.
Gifts wrapped up, oh what a sight,
Laughter bouncing through the night.

Celebration in Every Heart

Mistletoe hung in the oddest place,
A cat takes a leap, what a grace!
Chairs wobble under festive weight,
While Auntie grins, oh, isn't this great?

Candles flicker as grandpa snores,
Cookies vanish, now who wants more?
The kids plot tricks with sparkling eyes,
Wrapping dad in ribbons, oh what a prize!

Carols clash on the family stage,
Off-key voices, let loose your rage!
Dancing socks and shoes askew,
Oh, how silly this Christmas crew!

Sparkle and cheer fill every spot,
But where's the punch? Oh! Not in the pot!
With every grin a joy ignites,
Turning chaos into pure delights!

Whispers of Winter Wonder

Frosty flakes fall with a twist,
Snowball battles can't be missed.
Giggling children race outside,
In their sleds, they take a ride.

Hot cocoa spills, what a thrill!
While marshmallows float, a candy hill.
Grandpa's stories make us laugh,
Who knew he'd share his wooden giraffe?

Pine cones painted with silly cheer,
We hang them high for all to hear.
Christmas sweaters, oh so bright,
Worn by folks who bring delight.

As laughter dances through the night,
We warm our hearts with every bite.
Whispers float on chilly air,
Winter wonder is everywhere!

A Yuletide Serenade

Snowflakes twirl like ballerinas,
Cups of cheer, and lots of peanuts.
Dad's in charge of cooking grace,
But who thought he'd burn down the place?

Sisters string lights in a tangle,
While brothers plan a raucous bangle.
With laughter echoing through the halls,
It's a circus before the calls.

Gifts are wrapped with wild designs,
A cat emerges from bright confines.
Mom says, "Where's the holiday glee?"
In the chaos, there's joy, you see!

Carols sung in humorous style,
With off-key notes that last a while.
As the night hums a festive tune,
We embrace the fun, not the gloom!

Embracing the Spirit of Togetherness

Socks mismatched, giggles abound,
Uncle Joe's hat is turned upside down.
Grandma's baking, and flour flies,
Elves sing loudly, what a surprise!

Tinsel tangled in the cat's tail,
Kids start plotting a snowball hail.
Laughter erupts as the cookies burn,
Hot cocoa spills as youth starts to churn.

A Canvas of Colors in the Snow

Snowman wobbles, carrot nose askew,
Red mittens roam, chasing the blue.
Painted skies, but instead it rains,
Children jump, splashing, while Grandma complains.

Snowflakes dance like they're in a show,
Hot dogs roast, with marshmallows in tow.
Colorful chaos on a canvas so bright,
Mixed with snowball fights—oh, what a sight!

Frosted Wishes and Merry Whispers

Whispers of secrets in the twilight glow,
Sugar-plum fairies dance, but oh, so slow.
Stockings hang awkward, hope they'll hold,
Fantasy wrapping around us like gold.

Mistletoe mishaps cause laughter to reign,
Kissing a grumpy cat brings only pain.
Dreams and giggles echo outside,
As the snow softly joins in the ride.

Journey of Kindness Under Moonlight

Under the stars, with laughter so loud,
Journeying home through a hyperactive crowd.
A pie flops over, oh what a sight,
But hearts are warm as we share this night.

A sleigh ride mishap? Just a bit of fun,
Chasing our shadows, we dash and we run.
Jokes fill the air, like snowflakes so bright,
Wishes exchanged, all wrapped up tight.

The Story of the Silent Night

Under the stars, wrapped in thick fluff,
A cow in the corner stole some of the stuff.
The shepherds all whispered, trying to peek,
While Mary just giggled, 'He's quiet, not meek.'

The angels were dancing, they gave quite a show,
But one tripped on wings, landing right in the snow.
A donkey just snorted, as if to comply,
In the glow of the night, oh my, how they fly!

Golden Moments in Silver Light

In the kitchen, the cookies were burnt to a crisp,
Dad said with a grin, 'It's a new Christmas lisp!'
The dog did a heist, snatching treats from the plate,
Mom chased him around, but they laughed 'til too late.

Outside, kids were bundled, all ready to freeze,
Building snowmen with style, but no one could please.
A bucket for a hat and a carrot that glows,
And one kid named Timmy, just used his old clothes!

A Symphony of Kindred Spirits

Gathered in circles, the laughter did swell,
Like a family choir, all ringing the bell.
Uncle Joe's off-key, yet we smile and we cheer,
While Aunt Sue just waltzes, with punch in her beer.

Fun hats on the table, a game of charades,
As Grandma gets going in her fanciest braids.
The room's filled with jests, uncontrollable glee,
And dad's telling stories, we plead, 'Oh please, three!'

The Blessing of Presence Over Presents

Gifts piled high, but the best's in the room,
A surprise visit from Cousin Bob with his broom.
His dance was a sight, we could hardly contain,
While kin sang along, 'No need for the pain!'

Wrapped in laughter, we hugged and we cried,
With warm hearts aplenty, we let humor glide.
The gift of just being, no need for the stress,
As we toasted with cheer, who needs fancier mess?

Warmth in the Cold: A Celebration

Snowflakes fall like confetti,
The kids scream with delight,
A snowman with a bow tie,
He's surely quite the sight!

Hot cocoa spills on my sweater,
Marshmallows dance in the mug,
Dad's trying to take a sip,
But the cat gave him a shrug!

Stockings stuffed with odd trinkets,
An old sock with a toy,
Grandma's famous fruitcake waits,
It's the highlight of our joy!

Laughter echoes through the halls,
As we all trip and fall,
Who knew that Christmas magic,
Could make clumsy feel so tall?

Love's Woven Threads of Hope

Grandpa's telling tales again,
Of reindeer on the run,
We laugh as he forgets the punch,
Just part of all the fun!

The Christmas lights are tangled,
Like Aunt Nancy's curls at night,
But we just hang them anyway,
To make our home feel bright!

A tree that's lopsided smiles,
With ornaments from last year's cheer,
Each one tells a funny story,
Of laughter shared and near!

With hugs and silly selfies,
We capture every scene,
In the fabric of our moments,
Love's our greatest sheen!

Twinkling Eyes and Open Hearts

Winter sparkles in our eyes,
The snowman holds a sign,
He points to all our mischief,
"Let's have a bit more wine!"

Cookies shaped like silly things,
Are left for joy to share,
And though they all come out wrong,
We say they're fine, we swear!

The cat slides down the hallway,
Chasing bits of ribbon gold,
A pillow fort's the new agenda,
In our cozy home so bold!

With every laugh and giggle,
We sing out loud and clear,
For in this prime-time frolic,
We keep our loved ones near!

The Melody of Joyful Laughter

Singing off-key by the fire,
Our carols are a treat,
Mom's dance moves are quite something,
As she skips on her feet!

Pine needles on the sofa,
Dad's lost his festive hat,
But no one seems to worry,
Even Fluffy's gone all fat!

Eggnog spills on Uncle Joe,
He grins without a care,
We cheer and tease him loudly,
There's joy in every air!

As laughter fills the moments,
And stories weave the day,
We know this strange magic,
Will never fade away!

Embracing Moments of Peace

On a couch so cozy, we all collide,
With snacks piled high, no need to hide.
The dog steals a treat, with stealthy glee,
As we snicker and munch, oh so carefree.

Grandpa drifts off, a snooze in his chair,
While kids play charades, a wild affair.
A shoe on the ceiling, a hat on the cat,
These silly moments, imagine that!

Laughter erupts with each quirky game,
Who knew family time could be so lame?
But in the chaos, we find our bliss,
Wrapped up in joy, we can't help but miss.

So here's to the mess, the giggles and cheer,
In our cozy abode, we hold it so dear.
For peace comes in laughter, in tissues shared,
A riotous peace, that shows how we cared.

Shadows of Light on the Snow

Snowflakes shimmer, a clumsy ballet,
As I trip on the sidewalk, oh what a display!
My nose is red, my hat's askew,
But the world is a wonder, all sparkly and new.

We build a snowman with a carrot for flair,
But he quickly gets lopsided, a comical scare.
With googly eyes, he looks quite absurd,
And that snowball fight? Oh, have you heard?

The neighbor's dog joins; he thinks it's a game,
He runs through our yard, just adding to fame.
With snow in his fur, he shakes it around,
Glorious chaos with laughter abound.

Through slips and through giggles, we dance in the light,
These shadows of joy make everything right.
So let it snow on, let the laughter flow,
In moments so silly, our hearts start to glow.

Stories Wrapped in Children's Laughter

In the corner sits a towering tree,
With ornaments dancing—oh, what a spree!
Kids laugh and whisper secrets so grand,
As they plot their escape with gingerbread in hand.

A paper crown sits crookedly on my head,
While they reenact tales of giants and bread.
Each giggle a treasure, each shout a delight,
In stories of mischief that stretch long into night.

The cat's hair is everywhere, a fuzzy old sprite,
As we toss crumpled paper, a hilarious sight.
With bits of the wrapping all over the floor,
These stories wrapped up, we can't help but roar.

So hang on to laughter, it's truly the best,
In these tales of delight, we're truly blessed.
May the joy never fade, let the merriment stay,
Wrapped in a blanket of giggles, we play.

The Glorious Return of Radiant Hope

A jingle of bells, I hear from afar,
It's Uncle Joe singing, off-key, bizarre.
With a sweater so bright, it blinds the whole room,
He claims it's tradition, but it feels like a gloom.

The lights on the tree sparkle, twinkle, and flash,
As if they're auditioning for a cabaret bash.
The cat swats at tinsel, all full of finesse,
Creating a scene that's a glorious mess.

Grandma's famous pie sits proud on the shelf,
But somehow she mixed in a shoe with the elf.
We taste her creation with a mix of dread,
And laugh till we cry while rolling in bread.

So here's to the laughs, the mishaps, the cheer,
For ridiculous moments make memories dear.
With hope shining brighter than glimmers of gold,
In our wacky adventures, we flourish, we hold.

A Symphony of Kindness

In the chaos of wrapping, what did I find?
A cat in the box, oh, how unkind!
With ribbons and paper all over the floor,
Our holiday spirit is hard to ignore.

The cookies went missing, the reindeer are sly,
They're breaking in early, oh my, oh my!
Santa's got some tricks, he's not playing fair,
With crumbs on the table, they haven't a care.

We sing off-key with a jingle bell cheer,
While Uncle Bob's snoring, oh dear, oh dear!
The music keeps playing, a festive delight,
'Til someone spills cider, what a hilarious sight!

In a whirl of laughter, joy fills the air,
Our symphony swells with fun everywhere.
So here's to the quirks that make our hearts sing,
Together we'll celebrate, let the joy bells ring!

Celestial Lights Above

Look at the lights up there in a row,
They twinkle like stars, just put on a show!
But wait, that's Aunt June with a glow on her face,
Wrapped up in tinsel, she's stealing the place.

The dog's got a nose for the holiday cheer,
He's unwrapped the presents, oh dear, oh dear!
With paper confetti all over the lawn,
It's a Christmas surprise, just wait 'til the dawn.

The finale is coming, a dance on the floor,
Grandpa's still thinking he's twenty once more.
The lights keep on sparkling, laughter's our guide,
With every silly moment, we beam with pride.

So raise up a glass to the mishaps we see,
For each little laugh's a true gift, you'll agree.
Under celestial lights, let our spirits align,
In this quirky celebration, everything's fine!

The Magic of Togetherness

Here we are gathered, singing out loud,
In our matching sweaters, looking quite proud!
But oh, what's that smell? Is the turkey on fire?
If it's burnt to a crisp, we'll still never tire.

The kids are all bouncing, with gifts in their hands,
While dad's stuck in traffic, with the popcorn he planned.

A sibling's prank goes awry with a splash,
Pudding everywhere — oh, what a gnash!

A magical Hobbit, with glittery flair,
Uncle Joe's reindeer, with more junk in their hair.
Together we giggle, and sometimes we fight,
But these wacky moments make everything right.

So here's to our family, the wild and the free,
In the chaos of cheer, it's the best place to be.
We wrap up the laughter, the hugs that we share,
With each funny moment, we know that we care!

Joy Unwrapped on Christmas Eve

The night is alive with a squirrel on the tree,
He's munching on ornaments, oh, can't you see?
We hang up the stockings, but what do we find?
A frog in a hat, how could he be so blind?

The kids are all bubbling, fighting for space,
As grandma's baked cookies that none can replace.
But wait! There's an elf with a gift, oh so grand,
And then he confesses, it was made by hand!

Oh, what a ruckus, with giggles and cheers,
As we count down the moments to ring in the years.
With laughter surrounding, we skip and we prance,
The cat steals a ribbon, it's a holiday dance!

Finally we settle, in a pile by the fire,
With warmth in our hearts, and saying what's dire.
So here's to the laughter that each year bestows,
In this wacky adventure, our joy freely flows!

The Promise of Tomorrow's Sunshine

Snowmen wear hats that are way too big,
Sledding down hills makes us dance a jig.
Hot cocoa spills, oh what a mess,
Laughter erupts, we couldn't care less.

Presents wrapped tight, with bows all askew,
A cat in the box thinks it's a zoo.
Mistletoe hung just above the door,
A kiss from the dog? We'll always want more!

Cookies left out for a jolly old chap,
Caught him snoring, took a quick nap!
Reindeer on rooftops, what a sight,
They're making a racket, oh what a night!

Tomorrow awaits with its glimmering light,
We'll chase our socks that have taken flight.
With giggles and glee, we march on our way,
For tomorrow, my friend, is another fun day!

Reminders of Love in the Air

Grandma's fruitcake, a family's delight,
Some think it's fruit, others just might.
Pine needles stuck in our holiday socks,
Wondering how they got there, like tiny little rocks.

Uncle Joe's sweater, a sight to behold,
In colors so bright, it's daringly bold.
Belly laughs echo, they bounce off the walls,
Together we're silly, we answer the calls.

Elves in the kitchen? Not quite, you see,
It's Aunt May and her infamous three-cheese brie.
With love in each bite, it's joyous and warm,
We feast like it's magic, a holiday form!

With hugs that are sticky and kisses that shine,
The air filled with cheer, it's all so divine.
In the chaos, we find just what we share,
Love and good humor, they're always right there!

Beneath the Boughs of Old Oak Trees

Under the boughs where squirrels play,
Singing a song to help pass the day.
Snowflakes falling like glitter from the sky,
We catch them on tongues and giggle, oh my!

Pine cones in pockets, we hear them all clatter,
Trying to bake cookies—what's that? A batter!
The dog steals a treat meant for Santa's delight,
We chase him around, what a silly fight!

Swirling in circles, we twirl and we spin,
Our joy is contagious, let the fun begin!
With laughter and cheer, we gather so near,
Beneath all the branches, our love is sincere.

The oak stands tall, whispering tales anew,
Of all of our giggles that grew and grew.
Together we smile, in the glow of the eve,
With joy in our hearts, we shall not leave!

Captured Smiles Beneath the Stars

Starlight twinkles like snowflakes in flight,
We'll gather our friends for a fun snowy night.
With cocoa and marshmallows piled high,
We'll toast to the moon, it's our sparkling pie!

In the yard we'll build a snow fort so grand,
Who knew we would wage a soft snowball stand?
Giggles and shivers and snowflakes that kiss,
Every laugh shared is a moment of bliss.

Beneath those bright stars, we scream and we cheer,
With playful mischief, we banish all fear.
Santa's watching us—can't he see the fun?
We're just kids again, here under the sun!

For in this sweet chaos, we find our way back,
To joys that we cherish, we never lose track.
Captured smiles shining, as bright as the morn,
A holiday spirit forever reborn!

Echoes of the Season's Spirit

Elves on shelves, giggling with glee,
Hiding in places, where could they be?
With reindeer games and laughter so bright,
They'll prank you all day, then take off at night.

The mistletoe's up, it's a sight to behold,
But watch out for Uncle, he's not too controlled.
A dance and a twirl, oh what a surprise,
When he steals a kiss, who can close their eyes?

Cookies are burning, the scents fill the air,
Grandma's sweet treats? They're beyond compare!
Yet just when you think it's a sugar-filled dream,
You find out too late—it's last night's whipped cream!

So gather 'round friends, bring your best cheer,
For laughter and joy are what we hold dear.
With giggles and winks through the frost and the snow,
Let's celebrate now, in the spirit's own glow.

The Gift of Starlit Nights

Under the stars, there's mischief afoot,
Snowmen are dancing, oh what a hoot!
With scarves flying wildly and hats askew,
They're planning a party, we haven't a clue.

While carolers sing in a voice not quite right,
There's laughter and giggles, they're taking to flight.
For when Christmas comes, so does the cheer,
And the fruitcake's still here from last year, oh dear!

With warm cocoa cups, and marshmallows too,
But oh, watch your nose—there's a marshmallow stew!
As family gathers amidst all the fun,
Just wait for the moment when snowballs are spun!

So toast to these nights, filled with laughter and light,
Through twinkling stars and the chill of the night.
Raise a cup to the joy that we hold oh so tight,
And to snowflakes that tickle our toes with delight!

Rejoice in Frosty Feasts

The turkey is singing, can you hear its song?
It's begged for a break, but it knows it won't be long.
With stuffing and gravy, oh what a delight,
But Aunt Mabel's casserole? It's quite the fright!

Smooth eggnog flows, out of cups it may spill,
A toast to the laughter, oh what a thrill!
But just when you think that the laughter won't end,
Here comes Cousin Fred, with a joke to offend!

With frost on the windows and snowflakes that fall,
Board games await, let the best win them all!
Just don't take a turn with the dice in a rush,
'Cause Uncle Joe's winning could lead to a hush.

So feast on the food, let your spirits fly high,
With moments of joy that are surely the pie.
As we gather and cheer, hand-in-hand, oh so tight,
Let's keep the fun rolling deep into the night!

Glimmers of Hope Beneath the Snow

Hidden beneath all that snowflakes and frost,
Lies laughter and joy, never truly lost.
The kids are outside, building their dreams,
While distant are sounds of their whimsical screams.

In blankets so warm, the cat has her nap,
While visions of sugar plums dance in her lap.
The holiday cards, all mismatched and bright,
Bring smiles and some giggles, what a funny sight!

The tree is aglow with each twinkling light,
But don't trust the tinsel—oh what a fright!
It's stuck to the cat, who's now in a race,
As she dashes around, leaving sparkles in place.

So cherish the moments, let laughter take flight,
For in this frosty season, the heart shines so bright.
Through giggles and fun, may your spirit now grow,
In the warmth of this time, where the joy's all aglow!

Footprints in the Freshly Fallen Snow

In snow so white, we slip and slide,
A snowball fight, our joy can't hide.
With frosty noses and cheeks so red,
We laugh and tumble, enough said!

The dog runs round, he thinks it's race,
He leaps and bounds with silly grace.
Each paw print looks like a silly map,
As we fall down, it's quite the mishap!

Snowmen wobble, their carrot nose,
Sunk in the snow, oh how it goes!
With scarves askew and a hat too big,
We stand back, giggling like a pig!

With cocoa cups, we share a cheer,
Hot marshmallows float, oh dear, oh dear!
We toast to snowflakes and sunny days,
Laughter grows in almost all ways!

Joy and Laughter in Abundance

The tree is up, with lights aglow,
Cookies baking, the dough's a show.
We dance around, with sprinkles flying,
Mom trips on a rug, oh how we're crying!

Presents wrapped, but dogs can taste,
They sneak a sniff, no time to waste.
With ribbons chewed, and paper torn,
We laugh so hard, we might just mourn!

Elf hats wobble, as we take a seat,
With laughter bubbling, can't be beat.
Around the table, stories unfold,
Of grandma's pie and adventures bold!

The joy just swells, it's got no end,
With family close, and hearts to mend.
Laughter rings, a tune so bright,
Oops! Someone's fallen in the light!

Embracing the Cold with Warmth Inside

Bundled up tight in coats too big,
A dance-off starts, let's see who digs!
With mittens on and boots that squeak,
We trip and spin, though we're a freak!

Snowflakes fall, like feathers in air,
We shake our heads, it's quite the affair!
With cheeks like cherries, we laugh and shout,
Why is it colder? We can't figure out!

In cozy nooks, with games we play,
Hot cider spillage, whoops! Hooray!
We snuggle close for warmth, that's true,
But the laughter here is the warmest brew!

With board games mixed and pizza crust,
We count our giggles, in laughter we trust.
In every room, the joy ignites,
Who's winning? Oh, that's all up for fights!

A Time for Reflection and Renewal

As the year ends, we're filled with cheer,
With resolutions we'll somehow veer.
I vow to eat less cake, oh dear,
But who can resist the sweets that appear?

We gather 'round for a year's review,
With tales of blunders and what we'll do.
My friend forgot to turn off the flame,
Oops! Thank goodness, it's all just a game!

With laughter shared, and eyes all bright,
We toast to mishaps that bring delight.
Here's to the moments that make us smile,
Let's cherish the trips, let's walk that mile!

Reflection done, we take a vow,
To keep the giggles, oh yes, somehow.
A promise made, and joy in store,
For silly adventures, and laughter galore!

Carols in the Crisp Night Air

We sing off-key in the cold,
Our noses red, and brave, and bold.
The dog howls back, he thinks he's grand,
While neighbors peek, they barely stand.

Our hats are bent, our scarves askew,
A snowman forms, he waves, it's true.
We laugh at all our silly tunes,
The carols drift beneath the moons.

The kids throw snow, aim at each other,
We're all aglow, that's how we smother.
Our laughter echoes, fills the night,
Like jolly elves, we're quite the sight.

Ice cream cones of frosty cheer,
We dine on treats, our fates are near.
In this cold, we find the zest,
With laughter loud, we feel the best.

Flakes of Kindness from Above

Frosty flakes fall from the sky,
They tickle noses, oh my, oh my!
Each flake brings a giggle or two,
As we all slip, then giggle anew.

The snowman's dressed in mismatched clothes,
A wooly hat and a big red nose.
He's quite the sight, he stands up tall,
But in a gust, he takes a fall!

We toss the flakes, we share a laugh,
With every slip, we find our Path.
Our joyful spirits fill the air,
As kindness falls, it's everywhere.

We build a fort, it's meant to last,
But down it comes — oh, what a blast!
In frozen fun, we carve our cheer,
While snowflakes laugh and disappear.

Joy Blooms in Every Heart

In a world of socks, mismatched and bright,
We wear them proudly, what a sight!
Giggles spill from every room,
As Grandma's cookies fill the gloom.

The tree's a mess with ornaments hiked,
A cat climbs up and gets quite spiked.
With glass balls rolling, down they crash,
We laugh it off, it's just a splash.

A game of charades erupts with glee,
Uncle Joe's moves, oh, can't you see?
We're all big kids, no doubt upstart,
For every mime, it fills the heart.

With silly hats and winks we play,
Our joy blooms bright, a festive bouquet.
In every flurry, we find our reprieve,
As family gathers, we all believe.

The Family Gathered

We crowd around the table wide,
Each plate a treasure, side by side.
Grandpa's stories tip and sway,
While Auntie's jokes make dinner play.

A toast with soda, hands in the air,
Uncle's faux pas, a laugh to share.
With children sneaking bites of pie,
And Grandpa winking as he sighs.

The dog's in there, he steals a seat,
A cheeky grin, what a treat!
In cozy corners, warmth will blend,
As laughter curls, we know no end.

We sing off-key, a family tune,
With voices blending, under the moon.
Through clatter and chatter, joy we find,
Together in warmth, our hearts entwined.

Hearts Alight

With twinkling lights and mischief bold,
We hang them low as stories unfold.
The cat it pounces, all tangled up,
In a string of lights — oh, what a pup!

Our hearts alight, a twinkle in eyes,
We share our secrets, like little spies.
With giggles echoing off the walls,
Like snowflakes drifting, the laughter calls.

We sip hot cocoa, marshmallows fly,
A playful battle, we're spirits high!
With every sip, our warmth does grow,
Through every spill, the smiles just glow.

So here's a toast, not with wine,
But with hot chocolate, oh so divine.
In the warmth we create, our joy will ignite,
As hearts alight on this winter night.

The Light Within the Season

Flip the switch, let lights display,
How did we end up in this fray?
A tangled mass, a beagle's game,
But once we're done, it's all the same.

Cookies baked, and flour flies,
Dad's in the kitchen, oh what a surprise!
Milk on his beard, a pie on his shoe,
It's time we got him a chef's debut!

Snowballs thrown at every turn,
Uncle Joe slips, it's our turn to learn.
"Keep your balance!" we loudly shout,
He aims back at us, and we scream and pout.

Yet laughter rings through winter's chill,
No place we'd rather go, nor other thrill.
With each mishap, we savor the cheers,
Growing together, fate bound by years.

Embracing the Winter Glow

In mittens prancing, what a sight,
Snowflakes landing, oh what delight!
Hot cocoa spills on a vibrant scarf,
Mom laughs and says, "That's your art!"

Sledding down the hill with grace,
Who knew it'd end in a snowman's face?
Joyous giggles, as we all face-plant,
A family portrait in disaster's chant.

Lights are twinkling on every lawn,
While Grandma winks, her antics drawn.
She's got a wink that makes the world grin,
A cookie thief with a big, toothy win!

So raise a glass, let's toast today,
To shenanigans that come out to play.
The laughter's bright, and we'll never tire,
With memories that spark our inner fire.

Glistening Yuletide Moments

The cat's in the tree, oh what a fright,
We've got ornaments stuck, it's a hilarious sight!
"Oh, look at Fluffy, the great feline star!"
She winks at us, while we sip hot jar.

Presents wrapped in paper sublime,
Oh wait, is this meant for me or for slime?
The dog just chewed through a corner or two,
And now our gift is a mystery, woohoo!

Carolers outside, hats askew,
Singing off-key, but still breaking through.
Their frostbitten faces in sheer delight,
The neighbors are peeking, in joyful fright.

We gather 'round the TV, tightly packed,
Watching bloopers of people "unstressed" and hacked.
With laughter and joy, we embrace every crack,
Creating our own fun as memories stack.

Boughs of Holly and Hope

Holly hangs from the door with cheer,
And Auntie insists, "A hug is near!"
Each bough is knotted with laughter and glee,
"Just try not to eat all the cookies," said she.

We dress the tree and argue a bit,
Debates on star or the angel to sit.
Finally, it's done, adorned with flair,
Now let's cover it up, not a hair!

The snowmen stacked in our front yard maze,
Each one drooping in unique ways,
A carrot nose and a silly grin,
Now watch out, they collaps - where do we begin?

With laughter ringing, the joy we find,
In the chaos and antics, our hearts entwined.
For in these moments through all of our woes,
We gather much hope with each bough that grows.

Milton Keynes UK
Ingram Content Group UK Ltd.
UKHW021241191124
451300UK00007B/178

9 789916 941041